The Crucible of the Miraculous

Also by Don C. Nix

Loss of Being
The Field of Being
Moments of Grace
Patterns of Being
Dancing with Presence

The Crucible of the Miraculous

Searching for Meaning in the Cosmos

Don C. Nix, J.D., Ph.D.

iUniverse, Inc.
New York Bloomington

The Crucible of the Miraculous
Searching for Meaning in the Cosmos

iUniverse books may be ordered through booksellers or by contacting:

iUniverse
1663 Liberty Drive
Bloomington, IN 47403
www.iuniverse.com
1-800-Authors (1-800-288-4677)

Because of the dynamic nature of the Internet, any Web addresses or links contained in this book may have changed since publication and may no longer be valid. The views expressed in this work are solely those of the author and do not necessarily reflect the views of the publisher, and the publisher hereby disclaims any responsibility for them.

ISBN: 978-1-4502-4226-4 (sc)
ISBN: 978-1-4502-4227-1 (ebook)

Printed in the United States of America

iUniverse rev. date: 07/01/2010

Dedication

To my lovely, exceptional grand-daughter, Joli Goard. I was present when you were born, and I thought my heart would burst in wonder. As I looked into your opening eyes, I was struck with the thought: "This is a very old soul." As you have grown in the years since, I have never doubted that thought. It seems to me that you look out into the world with a steady, direct gaze, and that you see the world as it actually is, in all its vast beauty and vast pain. I know that you have a brilliant future, and I know that you will make a deep contribution to this turbulent, confusing planet. Knowing you and having you as my grand-daughter has been one of the highlights of my life. Thank you for being you, and thank you for loving me. With great love from your

Far
Brynhoffnant, Wales
May 29, 2010

Contents

Introduction

A new understanding of reality is forming, and that understanding will include meaning at the heart of things. The physicist David Bohm added meaning as a third primordial element to Einstein's famous equation, E=MC2, which focused on energy and mass as the components of the universe. Bohm's addition of meaning is destined to etch itself into human consciousness in the years ahead. The view of the universe as a dead, material machine, formulated 400 years ago following the work of Newton and Descartes, is eroding before our very eyes.

The problem is that we have no idea how to approach the study of meaning in the universe. We have only the worn-out visions of traditional religion and traditional science, and neither is adequate to the task. Science is not framed to investigate invisible realities. Religions involve, for the most part, projections of human experience. The one thing that is certain is that the universe is nothing like a human. It functions in its own idiosyncratic way, more as a living, intelligent Field than a larger-than-life human being. Though It is Itself invisible, Being has the mysterious and disconcerting power of throwing up material worlds and populating them. Our minds are just beginning to wrap themselves around this reality.

Poetry is intrinsically connected to meaning. Poetry is the record of an explosion of inner experience, a momentary, evanescent convergence in the mind that, if not recorded, vanishes back into the restless pool of consciousness. A poem can deepen and crystallize an inner experience of meaning. Once recorded, the poem makes it possible to return to the excavated experience later and perhaps build on it.

At a deeper level, poetry is Being turning to regard Its own qualities and processes. Both poetry and Being are infinitely mysterious. The 81 poems in this little book chronicle the author's struggle to evolve into new consciousness of these realities. Derived in part from the latest thinking in quantum physics and in part from the ancient thought of Hinduism and Sufism, the poems have their origin in the modern search for meaning and reality at the Macro level.

1

I am forged by fire.
I have spent decades
in the crisis of becoming.
Now I am
what I will be,
and I can raise my head
and look around,
in astonishment,
at this Crucible of the Miraculous.

2

We live our lives
in simmering angst,
leavened by moments
of joy.
We hide our pain
from ourselves and others
and pretend
it's all O.K.
Occasionally it reaches
crescendo,
and things get bad,
and we need help.
Then fear falls back
to low and constant.
We do our best.
We live our life.
This is our human lot.

3

I need to know,
if you please,
if I am valued here.
I need to have,
if you possibly could,
proof that I belong.
Just being here is not enough.
Just breathing air
won't do the job.
If I'm to stretch
and reach for You,
I need to know just why.

4

I am not alone here
as I lie in bed
in the middle of night,
my mind all abuzz with life.
I search for the Other
that I know is here,
but I cannot see
my Host.
It's enough to know
that It is here,
inside my head,
inside my room.
Tomorrow, I'll resume
my life,
but I'll remember this.

5

The wave is coming,
a tsunami of change.
I can hear its roar,
I can feel its spray.
The ground is trembling,
the trees shrink back,
the world is holding
its breath.
It's still in the distance
and cannot be seen,
but I know that
it is coming.

6

Slowly
and painfully
we ascend.
The Universe
is unfolding Itself
as expanding and deepening
consciousness.
We are learning,
perhaps,
not to hurt
each other
so much.
Imperceptibly,
we are turning toward,
and realizing,
that we are one with
the rising Sun.

7

The earth may move.
The seas may rise.
Fire may fall
from the skies.
We tremble
as our destiny
comes slowly into view.
Humbled,
chastened,
and fearful,
we search for a
way forward
that is not filled
with death.

8

I've tried my best
to play the game,
to get the cheers,
to win the gold.
I'm wondering now
in this final set,
and at this very late date,
who kept the score,
who tallied the points,
and why was the game
so hard?

9

Early morning.
My favorite time.
The world wakes up.
Another day.
The Light comes back.
The Dark recedes.
My hopes and dreams
self-resurrect.
With questions still unanswered,
I launch myself
into another day.

10

When I can't reach You
the world is dense,
my mood is black,
my problems immense,
my capacities nil,
my fears everywhere.
I wait,
patiently,
for the day to break.
I wait,
patiently,
for the Light to enter.
I wait,
patiently,
for the touch
of Your Sublimity
to bring my heart
back to life.

11

Something is moving me
through my life,
exchanging my cells,
and breathing my breath,
and beating my heart
and teaching me lessons.
Slowly and invisibly
It is taking me back to Being,
where I started
so long ago,
as an impulse
toward new life.

12

I seem to be made
of layers
through which I ceaselessly move,
each a realm
of itself,
complete and distinct,
and unlike all the others.
I move through the day
in the dense world.
Then I float,
weightless and transparent,
in a sea
of gossamer mind.
Occasionally,
and perhaps now,
I expand into space
to encounter the Boundless,
and Vastness
and Mystery.
I leave the earth and,
in a moment of wonder,
enter the swirling galaxies.

13

I am a creature of moments,
diverse,
unique,
and surprising,
each a tapestry
of a thousand threads
weaving together to make
a confluence
that will never
happen again.
I think of myself
as coherent.
I think of my life
as a line,
but the truth
is a bit more complex.
I am a thing
of encounters,
of merging patterns,
and meshing forces
coming together
in each moment
to unfold Something
hidden, sublime.

14

Beneath the skin of the world
a powerful Life resides,
awake and aware,
luminous and shining,
It unfolds Itself
as a vast,
intricate, patterned
Cosmos,
pouring Its
livingness and brilliance
into a waiting world.

15

Inside my head I have right now
a pool of sacred space,
invisible Livingness,
charged with Being
in Its purest, transparent form.
I think,
I see,
I make my plans
through the prism
of this pool,
that for this briefest
time is mine
as an astounding gift.

16

I am a hero, it seems,
though no-one knows it
but me.
I have spent decades
in fear,
facing the possibilities
of premature death,
and nuclear war,
and cancer,
and car-wreck,
and now—
heart attack and stroke.
I have courageously
pursued my life anyway,
steadfastly,
stubbornly,
in the very face
of fear.
Now that I think of it,
there are billions of us
on this planet,
each living our life
in spite of fear—
heroes all.

17

I am a collection of vast forces
constellated at the moment of birth,
thrown forth from the sea
of invisible Life,
in perfect replication
of the Macrocosm
at that very particular instant.
There are billions like me,
each perfectly unique,
each perfectly formed,
each walking the streets
of the city,
each an expression
of burgeoning Life.

18

"Make of yourself a light,"
the dying Buddha said,
and his frightened disciples asked
"What can it possibly mean?"
But it's clear to me
at this moment
what the dying Buddha meant.
"Take your new mind
with my teachings
into the turbulent world.
Stand as a beacon of light,
and shine,
shine,
shine."

19

With each breath that I draw
my life grows shorter,
my time on Earth wanes,
my drama recedes.
I am a disappearing act.
I am the Cheshire Cat.
I am vanishing incrementally
until,
sometime soon,
in a burst of light,
I will leave entirely,
off to become the galaxies.

20

My life is inflected toward soul.
My crises and dramas
uncover my strengths,
revealing what's always
been there,
in potential,
in the soul,
waiting for the daylight.
I am caught in alchemy,
as the pain of my life
unfolds my self,
unfolds my soul.

21

I am nobody,
struggling,
as always,
to be somebody.
It's not a bad thing
to be nobody,
but I've always
wanted more.
Now I've lived
long enough to realize
that though nobody
I'll remain,
it really doesn't matter
because I'm also everything.

22

Beneath the crust of the world
a luminous Radiance lies,
shining,
shimmering,
expressing Its way
to the surface,
and throwing
the world into motion,
with meaning,
with significance,
with drama,
and an endless
cycle of becoming.

23

My dreams seem somehow always
to bump into necessity,
taken apart by forces
that I don't expect
and cannot foresee.
I am impacted by powerful currents
that converge to create
this unfolding,
surprising
drama
that I have learned
to call my life.

24

Life is a layered thing.
We spend too much time
on its outer crust,
bewitched by
the mundane and superficial,
and enchanted
by our problems.
Beneath the turbulence,
however,
unseen patterns are unfolding,
deep, powerful and dynamic,
taking us to places that
we cannot even imagine.

25

Wandering through the Cosmos,
looking for truth,
Reality flares momentarily,
then vanishes behind appearances.
I am a fragment of consciousness
lost in the mystery
of metamorphosing Sublimity, and
searching,
searching,
searching,
to find the way back home.

26

I am a walking reef
of tiny, living forms—
particles, molecules, cells—
aggregated temporarily
into this body
that I know so well.
We (and I use the plural advisedly)
get along well,
each of us doing our job,
making our contribution,
playing our part,
to keep this ecosystem
that is me
alive and walking the earth
for just this brief moment of time.

27

We are swimming for a lifetime
in living, generative space,
thrown up as idea in matter
to dance the dream of life.
We arise as a something
in the world
to have our day or decades,
then vanish
in a blaze of light
back into the shimmering Sea.

28

I hear the steps behind me
of the great, dark God of Death.
I feel His cold,
I feel His depth,
I feel His breath.
Shiva, take me
when you choose.
I have had my
magnificent time.
I will go
smiling and grateful
into your Cosmic laugh.

29

Our children come through us,
not from us.
We contact them briefly,
in wonder.
They pass through our lives
too quickly,
on the way to their destiny.
For awhile
we are charged with their care,
and then we must let them go.
Like ourselves,
they are on a great journey,
passing through form and matter,
on their way back
to Living Light.

30

In the course of a day
I move through the realms,
from the flat, hard world
to invisible Life.
I seem to be pushed
by an unseen hand
from layer to layer
of Reality's web.
I'm not in control here,
as much as I'd like,
I voyage in realms,
along for the ride.

31

The door to my soul
swings open.
I am filled with bliss
and tears.
I am seeing the world
through new eyes.
I am seeing through
my fears.
I am seeing the world
with an open heart.
I'm seeing what's
really there.
It has always been there,
it seems,
but I have been blind
for years.

32

I don't remember choosing
to come to this world of pain.
I found myself already here,
embodied in protoplasm,
before I was aware of it.
I thought I might find
some harmony,
and I searched for it
high and low,
but it's elusive and disappearing
in the chaos of pain and strife.
The world is a crucible,
it seems,
designed not to be serene,
but to pound us and burn us
unceasingly,
to lead us to Life unseen.

33

Moment by moment
Being puddles into form,
as currents and threads
come together
to create astonishing Life.
Whirlpools form,
the unique arrives,
form and structure emerge
where there was nothing before.
What is this shimmering Force
that lies just beneath the crust,
mysterious, fecund, and dynamic,
with the power to populate worlds?

34

We spill our presence
into the world.
In adding our flavor
we're both process
and product,
threads in a Force
that is constantly distilling
pain into consciousness.
Our threads interweave
with others.,
as we effloresce our way
back to Living Light.

35

Of how many levels of life
are we completely unaware?
What to eat for dinner eclipses
matters of Cosmic import.
We stumble through life
asleep,
blind to miracle,
and absorbed
in viewing our toes.
What would it take
to shake us awake,
to make us sit up
and notice
that the Cosmos is a
living,
spinning,
shimmering
Force,
exploding Itself,
right now,
into matter?

36

I am working my way
back to Living Light.
I have had my day.
I have walked the earth.
I have lived my life
in a torrent of pain,
and joy,
and drama,
and wonder.
Now I turn my face
to the East.
awaiting the rise
of a fresh, new dawn.

37

Consciousness is the matrix.
Bodies come and go.
Beneath the life of Earth,
metamorphosing,
spinning,
roiling in its chaos,
a Cosmic Mind abides
in perfect silence
and stillness.
As It thinks,
worlds are born,
stars explode,
galaxies collide,
as nothing becomes something—
a miraculous, material universe.

38

We spill our pain
into the world,
while trying not
to have it seen.
In human life
we're hit full-face
with death,
and loss,
and failure
and disappointments
irredeemable.
We pick ourselves up
and try again.
We keep on going,
shriven of our illusions,
and waiting,
waiting,
waiting,
for the lessening
of our pain.

39

Life keeps throwing us curveballs.
The unexpected hangs in wait.
We respond as best we can
with the resources
we have on hand.
Sometimes we salvage the day.
Sometimes we're crushed by defeat.
We float on a flood
of possibilities
that dissolve,
in the end,
into space.

40

I can see more each day
as I open to Essence within.
I see through the world
to the realm of light
in moments
when I'm awake.
The world is a crust
on the surface of Life.
The glory is all within.
When my eyes are opened,
my boundaries dissolve,
the heaviness lifts,
and the radiance flares.

41

We are idea walking,
billions of us
on the earth,
each a coherent composite
of characteristics,
and experiences,
and destiny.
We live out
our life cycles,
both modular
and unique,
each expressing the thrust
of the unseen Force at work.

42

We are not yet
what we will be.
A new kind of mind
is blooming
that will take us
to realms now unseen,
beyond separateness,
beyond isolation,
beyond loneliness and despair,
to the knowledge
that is coming like thunder,
that we and the Cosmos
are one.

43

An earthquake is coming now,
but it won't be seen or felt.
It's an earthquake
of mind and perspective
that will shake us,
and shatter us,
and leave us trembling,
as we evolve
into the certainty
that we float
in a Living Sea.

44

Each day the sun returns
to spill its warmth
on the waiting earth.
Living Light arrives,
is eaten by
the grateful plants,
and turned at length
into their lives.
This happens every day,
but we,
unconscious and preoccupied
with our eternal little crises,
fail to look up and notice.
We should fall on our knees
in wonder
at this miracle of the light.
All life on earth
depends on it,
including us.

45

Our consciousness is expanding.
Our new awareness is blooming.
We are realizing,
slowly but steadily,
that Earth is more than resources.
It's a living, pulsing Being,
supporting,
sustaining,
and nurturing
every moment of our lives.
We are evolving our way
to a new mind
that realizes clearly
the miracle of the earth
and its place in the Cosmic Sea.

46

Early morning.
The birds and the trees
are welcoming
the return of
exuberant sun,
giving its substance,
shedding its warmth
and spreading its life
over a waking earth.

47

Each moment arrives uniquely,
a confluence of forces unseen.
Life unfolds itself
before my astonished eyes.
It burgeons.
It blooms.
It explodes
with the power
of unseen Light.

48

In the spreading dawn
I try to wake myself up.
I try to push
through my edges.
I try to expand myself
to touch the
vast flow of Life.
I reach for
the Brilliance
that I know is here,
throwing up
this pulsing dawn.

49

I was born in the Big Bang,
pulled by glittering galaxies
from depths of living night.
I blew to Earth
from exploding stars,
and found a home
in watery depths.
I grew myself—
eyes, heart, and spine—
and came out onto the land.
I stood and roamed and hunted and
compounded my little brain.
I learned to think,
and speak and build.
I grew to rule the earth.
Then I forgot my origins,
and turned in on myself.
Now I look at the stars
on a jet-black night,
with no inkling of my birth.

50

The solid world
is not.
The empty space
is not.
We live in a web
of illusion,
unconscious of
glory blooming.
In moments,
when the mind stops,
we wake to
strangeness walking,
seeing through
the skin of life
to Mystery
at its core.

51

The Hindus call it Maya,
the conjurer's trick
that is our world.
Nothing is what it seems.
That solid stone is space.
That eternal mountain is temporary.
That empty space is dense
with roiling, bubbling life.
We need new eyes to see
beneath the crust of life,
the efflorescence of the Sublime
emerging as our world.

52

The arc of my life continues.
I am not finished yet.
I still discover myself,
and see myself,
and understand myself,
in unexpected ways.
I am,
at heart,
an unfolding
of mystery, potential and space.
Where I will finish
is anyone's guess.
Surprise still lies in wait.

53

We are each
an unfolding miracle,
asleep but walking the earth.
We burgeon forth
from Mystery,
with pain,
and joy,
and wonder,
to dance our dance,
to live our lives,
and to work our way
back to Living Light.

54

In the early dawn
I blow through my edges.
My heart merges
with the trees.
I am lifted,
momentarily,
out of myself.
I am one with
all that I see.
I have waited for this,
patiently,
and now it has finally arrived.
I am larger than I thought.
I reach all the way
to the sky.

55

We are mesmerized by our thoughts.
They come and go
in the silent space
just behind our eyes.
We rarely look
at this magical pool
that hosts the thoughts
in our head.
Our minds are part
of a marvelous Sea,
a Sea of Sensitivity
that is
alive, awake and aware.
This is the realm
of the mind
of the Cosmos,
a living, conscious Sea.

56

I never expected to live this long.
I thought I would never be old.
Each phase of my life
was etched in light,
bursting and blooming
deepening and expanding.
So much experience.
So many joys,
and griefs,
and fears,
and triumphs,
and failures,
and wonder.
Now I look back
with curious eyes
to see what the through-line was.
Why did I come here?
What did I learn?
And what was that all about, anyway?

57

I've stumbled my way through my life,
confused and disoriented,
unconscious and blind,
without understanding,
and deeply concerned
with trivia.
I felt like the wolf
was at the door
for seventy-one years
and more.
It was never true,
I think.
I conjured the drama.
I conjured the angst.
I felt deeply afraid
when there was no wolf.
I'd like to have had
a play-bill,
a program of acts to come,
but it seems to be
part of the bargain
to stumble our way
back home.

58

We live for moments of sweetness
that come too seldom, too few.
We're caught in a tumult of whirling and fears,
and we're separate most of the time.
Then suddenly,
sometimes,
unheralded,
a marvelous sweetness appears.
We're startled and moved
to merge with the depths
of something tender and grand.
Our heart opens then to Great Life
and perhaps there are a few tears.
We are truly alive in that moment.
We are truly beyond our fears.
We could do worse than lie in wait
for the sweetness of Life to appear.

59

We are prone to idealize life,
and our lovers,
and our family,
and our children,
and ourselves.
We'd like it all to be perfect.
We pretend it could be that way.
We are shocked when reality
seeps up through the cracks,
to destroy our castle of dreams.
The ideal is really a blinder
that keeps us from seeing real Life,
with its crises and triumphs,
its pain and its joy,
the sweetness of Life in its all.
When we're in the cocoon of illusion
we're primed for a really bad fall.

60

Life is miraculous
just as it is,
but we fail to perceive
its glory.
We conjure ideal illusions
to replace the glory we missed.
We push our real life
into the ideal,
and we think that our life
will be all Spring.
We avert our eyes
from the shadow,
but we're playing a risky game.
Sooner or later
Life cracks the ideal
in the crucible of the real.
Then we are brought violently
down to earth,
and the pain can be severe.
It's the price that we pay
for illusion,
for departing the
realm of the real.

61

When my mind is small
I am lost,
trapped in a superficial world.
I wait for the Light
to reappear,
while I'm lost
in desolation.
Meaning has fled my earth.
Depth has abandoned me.
In these moments
of loss of Being,
I am lost
while still trying to see.

62

I want to die
while I'm still expanding.
I want to leave
while I'm still full of life.
Don't box me in
with infirmity.
Don't narrow my options
with age.
Take me out of this world
still resisting.
Give me choices until the end.
Give me vigor, clear mind and vision.
Take me out of this world
with my rage.

63

Look at the world
through eyes of oneness
and you'll see
a different world—
a web of Being,
inter-laced,
moving and changing,
unfolding Itself
relentlessly,
into Its future shape.

64

We pull ourselves
forward with dreams.
They are windows
into our soul,
expressing our deepest yearnings,
in code,
for the soul's desire
to complete itself.
We must separate
our dreams and our hopes
from our idealizations of life.
We must stay with the real
while we still have our hopes.
Clarity lies this way.

65

Life is a riddle
of days and nights.
Solving it takes
a lifetime.
We search for a clue
about what to do,
but the universe
is withholding.
Then sometimes,
it seems,
almost by chance,
we stumble onto our path.
With the wind
at our back
we can sail for awhile,
becoming more of who
we are,
who we've always been.

66

We only see a fraction
of what's around us here.
The Field is rich and layered,
but our eyes are not designed
to penetrate the outer crust,
to reach the depths,
to feel the brooding Presence
in the realms of the Unseen.
If we know that
there is more here
than our senses can detect,
it won't take us clear to Being
but it's a promising start.

67

We are trapped in our heads today.
We think that we can think our way
to realms of Paradise,
but the mind is not the tool
to touch the vast Unseen.
It's done with the cells and the heart,
by developing sensitivity
to nuances of sensation
and gradations of subtle feeling.
Turn toward the body
and wake it up.
Sense into your inner space.
Connect with your deepest inner self
and enter a brand new world.

68

Life unfolds itself into the future
before our astonished eyes,
as the restless, shifting Cosmos
reveals Itself in form.
Metamorphosis all around us.
Erosion takes things out.
The fresh and new emerges.
Inspiration strikes,
cities are built,
people we love disappear.
We are caught on the crest
of a moving wave,
while yearning to find
something stable.
Relax,
lose your fears,
and enjoy the ride,
if you are willing
and if you are able.

69

Under a cloudy sky
Life broods
and waits for the sun.
The world is holding
its breath
to see what is next
in this cavalcade
of wonders.

70

Creativity flows through me,
not from me,
and I realize
it's not really mine.
The impulse to craft
something new and fine
is rooted in Power
so deep and profound
that a glimpse of It
stills my mind.

71

The world is made of particles,
each a tiny, whirling galaxy
of luminous, dancing life.
Each form is an aggregation,
particles in a cluster,
shining with brilliance
and dancing their way
into the waiting world.
The world is emerging magically,
and temporarily,
from a void of Living Night.
Miracle is abroad
in the Cosmos,
and we are Its end result.

72

I look out into the world.
I sense its living heart.
I see the vast complexity
of which I am a part.
It is efflorescing miracle
that I am allowed to view.
I am cosmos viewing Cosmos.
I am mind perceiving Mind.
I am life perceiving Life.
I'm both inside and outside
this Mystery,
this emergence of the new.

73

Ego, ego, ego,
what am I to do with you?
Don't you ever get tired
of craving applause?
Don't you ever
want something deeper?
Always invested in image.
Always trying to look good.
Don't you want to be free
of the limited me,
and leave the whole sideshow behind?
Don't you know that your push
to always be seen
is blocking the job at hand?
How can I expand,
be as big as I can,
when you're rooted
and mired in
a self-absorbed plan.

74

I'm a flower
blooming in Vastness.
I'm an acorn
seeking the Light.
I push up through
the humus of living,
trying to expand,
stretching my limits,
seeking to become
that which I
was meant to be,
to do that
for which I came.

75

We arrive in a burst of freshness.
With wonder we meet the world.
We grow and we change
in a patterned way,
as we travel the arc
of our turbulent lives.
We encounter the world
and are swept up
in the frenzy of movement and dance.
When the music slows
we look backward.
We can now see our life as a whole.
Then the wonder from
long ago reappears,
and recreates itself in our heart.
We catch our breath
at the beauty and pain
as we look back across the years.

76

New life blooms in the world,
emerging from
the depths of invisible Mystery.
Goats appear and act like goats,
and never, never like cows.
We live in the midst
of patterned life,
with beauty and meaning,
brilliant and shimmering,
perfectly organized,
perfectly coherent,
perfectly collated.
We're blind to it all.
We take it for granted.
If we could just open our eyes,
and take in the strangeness and order,
wonder would strike us dumb.

77

We are born in uniqueness,
thrown up to pursue a soul-task
designed just for us.
We have to search for and find it
and that's not easy,
or assured.
It's our goal and our purpose,
our evolutionary sign-post.
It's the source of our meaning,
and our thread in the unfolding
of the tapestry of Great Life.
It's that for which we were called forth.

78

We surf forward into the future,
anxious,
disarranged,
in despair,
at the crest of a great wave of time
that relentlessly moves us
toward our death.
It's part of the bargain
that brought us here.
We can't avert our eyes.
It stays with us in the moments
of tenderness,
and beauty,
and meaning,
and depth,
that move us to joyful tears.
Our only course is gratitude.
Live fully and
develop your heart.
Fully see the miracle
you've been given,
and move boldly past your fears.

79

Whirl is not King in the universe.
Life is not a dervish dance,
unless we allow it to be.
A silent, still Order exists down below,
of wonder and meaning and depth.
By moving too fast,
and straining too hard,
and having too much to do,
we stay on the surface in chaos,
and miss the sacred realm.
Slow down and wake up to Life,
or the turmoil will never cease.
Our passport is,
now and forever,
silence and stillness and peace.

80

The world spins awake
each morning.
Life rouses to dance
each day.
Sun enters stage-east
to pour its bright life
on a grateful and waiting Earth.
The birds are ecstatic.
The trees celebrate.
The flowers turn sunward
to follow its course.
Creation bursts out all anew.
The humans are all inside
brushing their teeth,
and sharpening their little ambitions.
Encased in separateness,
they are too busy to notice
we are swimming in miracle.

81

Put Your arms around me.
Extinguish my little mind.
Pull me into
Your beating heart,
And merge me with Your grace.
For a moment or more
let my life soar
into the vastness of space.
I'm here,
I'm alive,
and I'm conscious.
Lift me out
of this limited place.